Across Three Generations

Bolton County Borough Fire Brigade 1700-1974

Peter Riley, Grad.I.Fire.E

Jackson Publishing & Distribution
Stockport, Cheshire, UK

First published in Great Britain in 2003 by
Jackson Publishing & Distribution
3 Gibsons Road, Heaton Moor, Stockport. SK4 4JX

© Peter Riley

ISBN 0-954581-00-8

Print & Design by Paragon Co. Ltd,
Stockport Tel: 0161 477 6645
www.paragonprinting.co.uk

Contents

Bolton Fire Brigade in the 20th Century   33

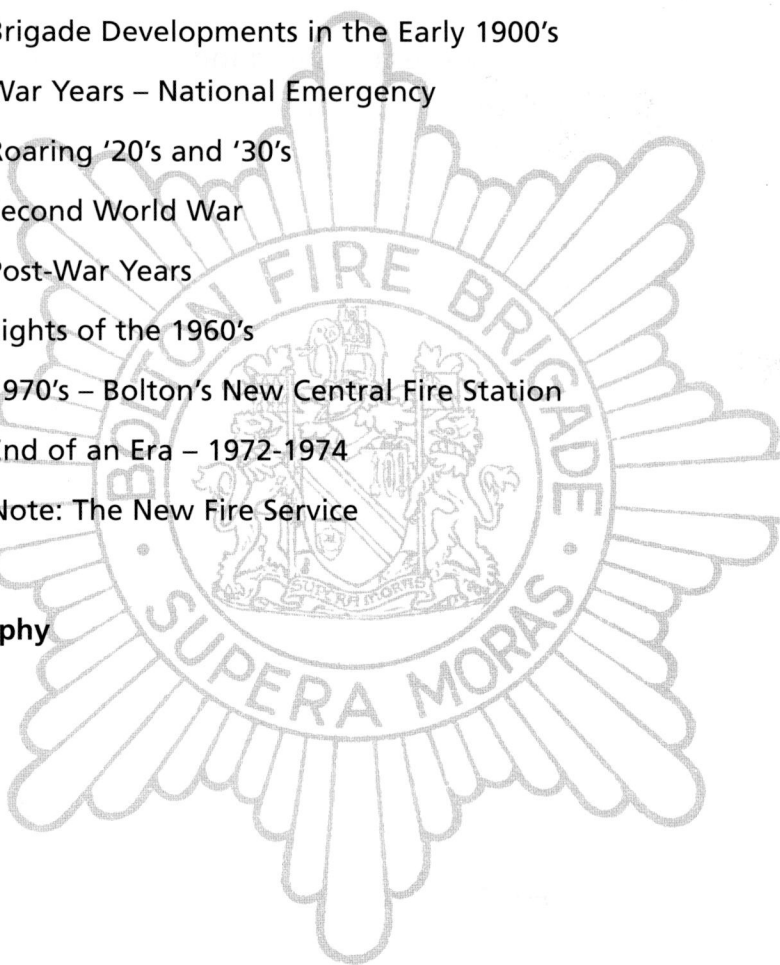

Bibliography

Acknowledgements

I wish to acknowledge the assistance, professional skills and guidance given to me by the following individuals and organisations, without whom this publication would not have been possible.

Mr. B. Dixon, *Q.F.S.M., M.I. Fire E., County Fire Officer and Chief Executive Greater Manchester Fire Service.*

Mr. G.H. Almond, *CBE, F.I. Fire E., F.R.S.H., F.I.P.D., (Retired).*

Mr. L. Gent, *Associate Editor Bolton Evening News, for the provision of photographic materials.*

Mr. B.D. Mills, *B.A., A.L.A. and staff – Bolton Reference Library for his assistance with the location of documentary sources.*

Past members and families of Bolton Fire Brigade. Service members and the people of Bolton for their generosity in donating photographs.

All members of G.M.F.S. Visual Aids Department for their assistance with the publication of this book.

Many thanks to all my family for their help and support.

Preface

The past three hundred years have seen many stories in the life of Bolton Fire Brigade and in turn, there have been many recorded reports of events and the people who have lived through them. Mine is not the first family to share a heritage of service in the fire brigade which stretches several generations. My family connection with Bolton Fire Brigade and the fire service runs through from Father, Son and Grandson. This connection is shared with many other families in Bolton including the following:

The Bentleys	-	Father and Sons
The Treachers	-	Father and Son
The Farrells	-	Father, Son and Grandson
The Hiltons	-	Brothers
The Rileys	-	Brothers
The Stallards	-	Brothers
The Beales	-	Brothers
The Loftuses	-	Father and Son

We are not the first family to share the stories of three generations in the fire service, and as the years roll by, we will certainly not be the last! Alongside this story, is a pictorial review of fire appliances and personnel over the last hundred years. The vast changes in appliances, equipment and the working conditions of Bolton's fire fighters will be seen, alongside some more general factual information providing an insight into the life of Bolton County Borough Fire Brigade and the lives of the people of Bolton over three centuries. I do hope that those who take the time to read and look at this historical account will enjoy the trip down memory lane.

Peter Riley *Grad. I. Fire E.*

Introduction
Like Father, Like Son;
The Fire Service Through Three Generations

The inspiration for compiling this pictorial and narrative account of the history of Bolton Fire Service over the past three centuries, originates in my family history and connections to service in the fire brigade across three generations which include: Edward Farrell my Grandfather, John Edward Farrell, M.B.E., M.I. Fire E. my uncle, and of course myself, as the grandson.

This book traces the history of the fire service through the eyes of these three generations of fire fighters.

Edward Farrell joined Bolton County Borough Fire Brigade in 1891 as an Auxiliary Fireman. Later, in 1899, he became a member of the full time staff, serving at Coronation Street Fire Station and, then, at the new station at Marsden Road. In 1912, he was appointed Engineer – part of his duties were to test and maintain the manuals, plus the steamer "Albert". He was promoted to Station Officer in 1920 and lived many happy years bringing up his family at Marsden Road Station and saw many changes in the service, including the development of manuals, the use of horses and steamers, and then new motorised fire engines. He retired in 1925 after 33 years service.

His son, John Edward Farrell, was born on Bolton Fire Station in 1904, and was appointed Auxiliary Fireman in 1922, aged 18 years. In 1926, he joined Manchester Fire Brigade, serving at City Stations and Brigade Workshops. He rose through the ranks to District Station Officer and, later, Inspector (M.F.B. was a Police Brigade). At 33 years of age he was elected to the Governing Council of the Institute of Fire Engineers. A short time later he was seconded from normal fire brigade duties to organise and train the Manchester Auxiliary Fire Service. His negotiations resulted in the establishment, at St. Joseph's Buildings, of the largest fire service owned training centre in the country.

He was promoted Deputy Chief of Manchester Fire Brigade and was on duty throughout the air raid blitz of Manchester. The city suffered 1,300 fires and 30,000 damaged buildings whilst Jack (John Edward Farrell) was fire fighting. His wife, Kathleen, was driving an ambulance in the city. There was no quiet family life in those days or nights. Jack was awarded the British Empire Medal in 1941, for his work in saving Manchester Town Hall during the Christmas Eve raids – the Brigade had 630 fires on the same night. In 1941, the Fire Service was nationalised. Jack was appointed Deputy Fire Force Commander No. 27 Area (Manchester). Eighteen months later, he was appointed Fire Force Commander No. 12 Area (Swansea). In July 1947, he was moved as Commander to No. 6 Area (Hull). In 1948, after the war, as the fire brigades were returned to Local Government, he was appointed County Fire Officer of the new West Riding County Fire

Service and, in that same year, became President of the Institute of Fire Engineers. He was a founder member of the Fire Service National Benevolent Fund and worked to ensure it had a good foundation on which to build for the future. In 1955, he retired after 32 years of public service. Jack had a long and happy retirement and was an active member of the Manchester Fire Brigade Retired Members Association until his passing in 1996.

Edward's grandson, Peter Riley, was born in Bolton in 1933. As my mother was born on Bolton Fire Station, and my uncle Jack Farrell was a serving officer with Manchester Fire Brigade, I heard many tales and stories about the fire brigade when I visited London Road Station. I was there when the daylight raids commenced. We were all removed to the station cellar until the all clear was sounded, however, the bells didn't stop ringing for hours!! After all the excitement and seeing the damaged city, we returned home to Bolton by train, which took many hours. Those visits and times bring back some happy memories of the Manchester Fire Brigade.

On leaving school, I was advised to train as an Engineer and I joined Mather and Platt Engineers as an Indentured Apprentice. I served in most departments and joined the work's Civil Defence Unit. In 1952, I joined Bolton Auxiliary Fire Service and served until I was called up in 1954 for National Service in the Army. After basic training, and passing a heavy vehicle driving course, I was posted to Manchester Fire Brigade Training Centre, London Road. My course instructors were Sub-Officers Allan Millner and Kenneth McKensie. I am happy to say that we are still friends.

My first posting was to 36 Army Fire Brigade Headquarters Station, Singapore where I attended many incidents in Army and Dock Installations, and more than enough grass bush fires. In 1956, I returned home to England and was discharged from active service. I applied for the post of Fireman with Lancashire County Fire Brigade, was accepted and posted to Stretford Fire Station. The first full week shift was the old 99 hours. I later attended the training centre at Morecambe Fire Station - my instructors being Sub-Officer Stan Platt and Sub-Officer J. Worthington. After passing out, I returned to Stretford to gain invaluable experience at one of the busiest stations in Lancashire.

In 1960, I transferred to Leigh Fire Station. I was now saving up to be married and the fire service pay did not help! I applied for the post of Leading Fireman at English Electric Fire Brigade, Preston. The salary was very good but the position did not come up to expectations. I applied for the post of Fireman with Bolton County Borough Fire Brigade and was accepted in 1961. I served at both stations in Bolton and in all departments at different ranks thus gaining invaluable experience as a Fire Officer at Bolton.

In 1974, Bolton Fire Brigade was combined with other local authority fire brigades to become the new Greater Manchester County Fire Brigade. In 1982, I was promoted to Assistant Divisional Officer and posted to Salford Fire Station. After a short stay, I was posted back to Bolton as Deputy Officer in charge, later to become Station Commander until my retirement in 1987 due to ill health. After 33 years service, I am still actively working with Greater Manchester Fire Service Retired Members Association and The Fire Service National Benevolent Fund.

In the beginning...
Fire Fighting in the 18th Century

The 1700's marked the beginning of Bolton Fire Brigade with the establishment of Bolton's first ever fire station. In describing the evolution of the fire service in Bolton during the late eighteenth century, the accounts which follow, provide a brief insight into the history of the Brigade and the working lives, pay and conditions of those who served in a fire fighting capacity during the early days of the service.

In 1780-90 the Bolton of this period was much smaller than today. It was, in fact, made up of two townships – Greater Bolton and Little Bolton. Both townships had their own manuals. The surrounding townships and hamlets of Breightmet, Darcy Lever, Lostock, Sharples, Halliwell, Tonge Moor, Heaton, Hulton, Rumworth were regarded as being separate. Fire cover for the township of Bolton was provided by the Royal Exchange Insurance Fire Brigade. As their business grew, the companies either supported the Provincial Brigades or, where the amount of business was smaller, provided equipment or financial subsidies to the municipalities or parishes in the region.

The inventions of Arkwright and Crompton brought about the rapid rise of the cotton industry in the region. With the building of large cotton mills, Bolton and district was to have approximately 387 mills and 28 bleaching and dying works, plus many other support services. Bolton rivers played a great part in supplying the water to drive the wheels of industry, with water wheels and steam engines and the large quantities of water required for the bleaching and dying of cloth. Due to the large numbers required to work in the cotton industry, the town's population expanded rapidly.

In 1792 an Act was passed, which laid the foundation for the town of Bolton as we know it today. The Act included provision for supplying the said township with water and providing fire engines and firemen. The trustees of the township appointed a 'Fire Engine Committee', its functions were to enquire into the value and size of a fire engine, how many firemen would be required for each respective size, and where engines could be purchased of the best construction and at the best price.

In 1795 a building called Barret's Barn was acquired for housing the fire engines and fire fighting equipment – this became Bolton's first fire station and as such, a significant land mark in the history of the fire service in Bolton.

Fire Service Development in the 19th Century

The 1800's saw significant development of the fire service in Bolton including the establishment of a uniformed brigade, the purchase of manual fire engines, the development of fire fighting procedures and the regulation of the Brigade via the township's trustees' committee. As one might expect, this period in the Brigade's development also witnessed numerous fires across the township of Bolton, a selected number of which are reported upon here, alongside the factual accounts which document the development of Bolton's Fire Brigade during the nineteenth century.

In 1802 the trustees of the township of Bolton authorized the erection of a building in Old Hall Street, in the yard of the old Work House, to accommodate the town's newly purchased fire engines. It was intended that this building would replace the old fire station located at Barret's Barn.

In 1808 Bolton's Fire Brigade really began to develop. In that year, a committee was formed from the trustees of the town, to consider and carry out to implementation, new rules and regulations pertaining to firemen and fire engines. The new rules do not appear to have materialized until 1812, but they were comprehensive and named the engines and crews – a Captain and three firemen to each engine. Two months later the committee was ordered to provide the firemen with jackets bearing a badge with the coat of arms of the town, thus indicating that Bolton had a uniformed Brigade. The newly established 'Brigade Rules' also indicated the establishment of an early pay structure for firemen, noting that, "… a premium of three (3) shillings be paid to the men whose engine should first play water on the fire; two (2) shillings should be given to the second".

In 1815 the firemen of Bolton were no longer restricted to fighting fires within the township, as during this year, it was decided to make a charge for the sevice of firemen and fire engines when used at fires outside the boundaries of the Bolton township.

In 1838 Bolton was granted the 'Charter of Incorporation', thus laying the foundation of the Municipal Administration which was to regulate local governance for the town. The trustees and citizens of the town must have regarded their fire service as a valuable civic asset, as in the same year, the Fire Brigade was included in the town's coronation parade marking the ascension of Queen Victoria to the throne – the latter being held in the new Market Square, which is now known as the Town Hall Square.

In 1840 a powerful manual fire engine called "Victoria" (no doubt named after the newly crowned queen) was recorded as operating from Little Bolton Fire Station – the Superintendent being a Mr. James Nicholson of Kay Street. The engine was the largest of the fleet recorded as in service during this period, requiring 42 firemen to operate it. In 1847 fire engines and equipment were transferred by the trustees of the old township to the newly established 'Bolton Corporation' who, under the Bolton Improvement Act, were empowered to provide fire engines and fire and police services. The functions of the Corporation for fire brigade purposes were carried out by a committee known as the 'Fire/Police Committee'.

The Star Concert Room Fire of 1852

In 1852, one of the main attractions in the Town, and of the North West, was the Star Concert Room, Churchgate. It was reputed to be one of the finest Concert Rooms in England. It lay behind the Star Inn and extended to Princess Street. It was three storeys high and measured 150 ft by 45 ft.

The ground floor of the building was used as a Brewing House, Stable Yard, Printshop and Workshop. The first floor was a Concert Room, the second floor was a Museum and Menagerie. The roof was flat and formed a promenade used on fine days to view the surrounding town and countryside. The south end was distinguished by a large ship's mast and rigging. The Museum contained many curios, including wax figures, stuffed reptiles and birds, models, geological specimens, works of art and a temple of magic. The Menagerie section included monkeys, squirrels, an Indian ferret and a two legged cat. The Concert Room extended the full length and breadth of the building and entertainment in the form of singing, living tableaux, light and heavy hornpipe, dancing and acrobatics was provided nightly.

On Monday, 12th July, the establishment closed for one week for redecoration. The following day seventeen painters, carpenters and labourers worked until 8 pm. The proprietor had intended to install a new gas lighting system which, that day, he had been to inspect in Liverpool. He arrived home at 10.15 pm and, with two friends, went up to the promenade roof to observe the distant electrical storms. He left a lighted candle at the foot of the stairs to facilitate their return. Some fifteen minutes later they returned downstairs and soon afterwards a passerby came in and told them that the museum was on fire.

The alarm spread along Deansgate and the fire was tackled by helpers using buckets of water, but it quickly got out of control and, in no time at all, the museum blazed from end to end. Here was a large building in flames, in the midst of an area thickly studded with cottages, shops, inns, and other buildings, embracing all the property on the south side of Churchgate and, as yet, no one had operated the fire plugs.

The Superintendent of the Fire Brigade was not, in the first instance, to be seen and, when he did arrive, he was of little value as he was in a state of intoxication. The operation of the fire plugs and hose was, to a great extent, taken over by the Police and several members of the Fire/Police Committee, other assistants included the Mayor and the Town Clerk.

The first three hose lines were got to work from fire plugs in Crown Street, Bank Street, and Deansgate. The "Victoria" belonging to the Corporation arrived and was set into the fire plugs opposite the Man & Scythe Inn, but not without first having been lifted over the hose lines which had already been laid out. The "Niagara", a large engine belonging to Messrs. Burton arrived and was placed at the rear of the Black Bull, Bradshawgate. The "Jessie" and "Bumble", belonging to the town, were also present. The "Etna, from Messrs. Ormrods Mill, was stationed near the Post Office. The "British Queen", from Messrs. Ainsworths of Halliwell, was stationed at the bottom of Wood Street. The two fire engines from Farnworth rattled along Bradshawgate – one was set in near the Vicarage, the other at the bottom of Oliver lane. The "Firefly", was also in attendance from Farnworth but was not used.

Several hose lines were taken through the Star Inn gateway to the Concert Room – one up the Corporation fire escape, which was placed in front the Star Inn, and another through the Swan yard. Further lines ran from Glazebrook Lane and Princess Street and one was taken into the yard of the Man & Scythe to protect that Inn.

By now the entire building was involved and threatened the whole of the property in Churchgate. The raging flames, combined with the numerous flashes of lightning had an awful effect. The mast and rigging on the roof blazed for a time and then fell crashing through the roof of a cottage in Glazebrook Lane. By midnight the building was gutted.

Thousands of spectators attracted to the scene lined Churchgate, Princess Street and Bradshawgate. The fire was got under control by 1.30am and damping down continued until 3 o'clock. Only the outer walls remained standing. The fire damage was estimated at £6-7,000. Also 60 workers were now without a job.

Following the fire, there were numerous complaints regarding the saving of property including, the delay between giving the alarm and any effective measures being taken, the general confusion amongst those who work the engines and the lack of crowd control. The noise, cursing and swearing of fire fighting personnel whilst engaged in the discharge of their duties was also commented upon, although this can scarcely be a matter of surprise when the Superintendent was drunk! He was in fact discharged the following day and the post advertised.

The tragedy was not to end there. On the Monday following the fire, the east wall fell into Wigan Lane, demolishing cottages there and killing three people.

Bolton's First Full-time Fireman

In 1853 the Fire/Police Committee was amalgamated with the Watch Committee during November. The Brigade, with the exception of war time National Fire Service, remained under its control until 1974. This meant that the Brigade was placed under the leadership of the Chief Constable. Additionally, a number of Constables alternated their police duties with periods of duty at the fire station. The Brigade therefore had a small number of men available for a quick turnout - this initial turnout was supplemented by Volunteer Auxiliaries who had to be called by messenger.

In 1867 some reorganisation of the Brigade took place involving the closing of Falcon Street Station and Old Hall Street Station, as this was on the site of the new Town Hall. The Brigade then moved to the Coronation Street premises. This was also the year in which the Brigade's Superintendent, Police Inspector Thomas Beach, was promoted to Chief Constable, and the man chosen to replace him in the Brigade was John Aspinall. He was a Captain (also titled "Keeper of the Engine House") and was promoted as a full time appointment to Superintendent at a salary of £78 per annum, plus house and rates free. So to John Aspinall went the distinction of being Bolton's first and, at that time, only full time Fireman.

Great Fire Engines of the Day

At this time Greater Bolton had manual fire engines named "Blucher", "Bumble" and "Jessie". The "Victoria" was still operating from Little Bolton. The following table gives some details: –

Name of Engine	Diameter of Cylinder	Stroke	Number of Men to operate	Height of Jet
VICTORIA	9"	8"	42	70'
JESSIE	7-1/8"	8-1/2"	36	70'
BUMBLE	6-3/8"	8-1/2"	36	70'

In 1855 a list of private fire engines included one from Firwood Bleachworks – this was built by Henry Hollins of Manchester in 1838. It is still going strong over 130 years later. It was donated to the Brigade in 1949 by the Bleachers Association, and restored by members of the Brigade and is now in the care of Bolton's Museum.

Fire station, Coronation Street, showing the steamer (Albert) 1868 and manual operated engine (Nelson) 1870.

In 1868 Bolton's first steam fire engine was delivered and named "Albert", no doubt in honour of Prince Albert, Queen Victoria's husband. The machine could carry a crew of eight, including the driver and engineer, and weighed 35 cwt. A double vertical action pump with 9-1/2" cylinder, Bolton's steamer was the first in the North West and was a Shand Mason model. Others soon followed at Manchester, Stockport and Rochdale.

Manchester had its own contenders who manufactured steam engines. William Rose Co. – they supplied steamers, escapes and fire hoses from their work in Salford. Others included Merry Weather, Braithwaites, and Erricson. In December a demonstration took place on the now Victoria Square, for all interested parties.

The boiler was lit and 100 PSI of steam was obtained in nine minutes fifteen seconds, suction hoses were set into a portable dam, and a 1-1/8" jet was first used and a height of 100' was reached. Further nozzles were used and all agreed the results were most satisfactory.

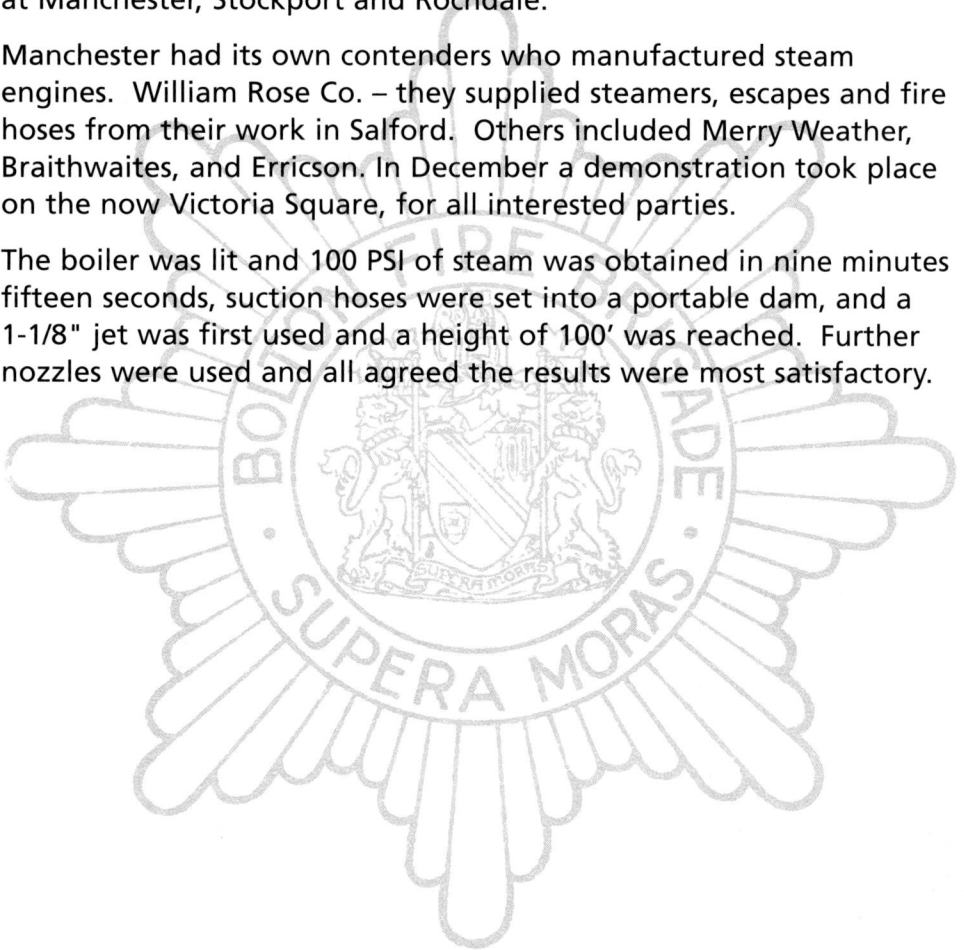

Fire Service Personnel and Equipment in 1875

Personnel

1 Superintendent

4 Engineers

24 Firemen

Wages Per Annum

Superintendent £90 plus house and Rates Free

3 Engineers   £8-6s-0d

1 Engineer   £5-4s-0d

17 Firemen   £7-6s-0d

7 Firemen   £5-4s-0d

Total Wage Bill for Year: £280-12s-0d

Equipment

Steam Fire Engine	1
Manual Fire Engines	2
Reel and Hose Carriages	2
Fire Escape Ladders	2
Stand Pipes	5
Suction Pipes	12
Delivery Pipes	20
Plug Pipes	1
Elbow Pipes	8
Hand Pumps	3
Canvas Hose	1,505 yds
Leather Hose	134 yds
Hydrants	726

Brigade Reorganisation 1875-1880

Following a serious illness Superintendent Mr John Aspinall died aged 44 years. He left a widow and nine children, for whom it was first said that no provision could be made as there were no funds available to provide pensions. Later some money was paid however, and it was proposed to buy some stock for a shop in order that she could earn her livelihood in the retail trade.

The post of Superintendent was advertised at a salary of £80 per annum plus house gas and coal provided. From a short list Mr. Robert Phillips, an Assistant Officer with London Fire Brigade was selected. Mr. Phillips, a native of Sussex and son of a Police Officer and Ex Royal navy. At the time of his appointment to Superintendent of Bolton Fire Brigade, it was hoped that with his vast experience (he had attended 1600 fires in London) he would soon increase the efficiency of the brigade. It would appear that this materialized, for in 1879, the members of the brigade presented him with an engraved helmet in recognition of a successful fire brigade competition. In 1877, 56 local mills had been connected by telegraph direct to the fire station. This brought about much needed improvements in reducing the time taken in calling the brigade. Prior to this, fire calls could only be sent, by messenger, on foot, or horseback. The telephone had only just been invented and was hardly known in this country.

A scheme for the reorganisation of the brigade was submitted and accepted. On 30th June 1880 the Fire/Police were relieved of their fire fighting duties and replaced by five firemen. Henceforth to be permanent full-time staff supplemented by the auxiliaries who had served in the Fire/Police Brigade. From 1st July 1880, permanent staff is recorded as follows:

Superintendent	R H Phillips
Deputy Superintendent	J Kennedy
Engineer	H J Batten
Engineer	T Hunt
Fireman	F Clarke
Fireman	D Healy

The first years of life, in the newly formed full-time Brigade, were to prove hectic, and on many occasions the Brigade was stretched beyond its limits. In fact, but for the ready support of industrial brigades, the high fire losses recorded at that time would have been even worse.

In September of 1880 a new steam fire engine was purchased and named Foster after the Chairman of the Watch Committee. It was supplied by Shand Mason of London, a no 4 patent Equilibrium Three pump Cylinders, each 8" diameter by 7" stroke capacity 3.83 and capable of delivering 900 gallons per minute. The travelling weight complete was 66cwt (poor horses) total cost £921-10s.

In June the Edison Telephone Company fitted up direct telegraph communications between the fire station and the dwellings of the superintendent and members of the permanent staff at a cost of £18-0s. and an annual maintenance of £4-0s.

The Fires of 1881

In 1881 a number of large fires occurred. Charles Taylor's Mill at Brownlow Fold (£35,000). Peter Crook's, Robin Hood Mill at Lever Street (£30,000) and Bull Field Mills (£10,000).

April brought the first recorded death of a Brigade member to be killed on duty. It was the practice at that time for the brigade to be drilled on the second Saturday of every month. A drill had taken place on the wholesale market facing the fire station in Coronation Street. Three Auxiliary Firemen were told by Superintendent Phillips to close the massive iron gates. As they were doing so, one of the flanges on the gate broke and the gate weighing more than a ton started to fall on the men. They ran, but one of them, John Byrne aged 23 of Parkfield, was caught on the back of the head as the gate fell on him. A crowd quickly gathered and lifted the gate off him. He was removed to the infirmary but died at 4pm.

hands). If it rang in the day time, the mother of the boy would have to go to his school and have a quick word with the master, who would give his permission for the lad to hare off to the several factories and mills where the auxiliaries worked. Night calls could prove a frightening ordeal, with the prospect of running through dimly lit deserted streets, anxiously seeking the white painted brick at the side of the front doors that indicated a home of an auxiliary. Occasionally the lads were chased though the streets by a suspicious policeman. Then came the hammering at the doors with a wooden mallet, and the blowing of a whistle, which often evoked a none too enthusiastic response from the residents. All this for a wage of four shillings per month, plus 1/6d for a fire call, reduced to one shilling if the call proved to be a false alarm.

The Brigade also assisted at fires in the surrounding areas, of Westhoughton, Tyldesley, Horwich and Turton and Superintendent Phillips submitted a scheme whereby the councils outside the borough would pay a fire brigade rate of under one penny in the £ and be entitled to Bolton's services, but nothing came of his proposal.

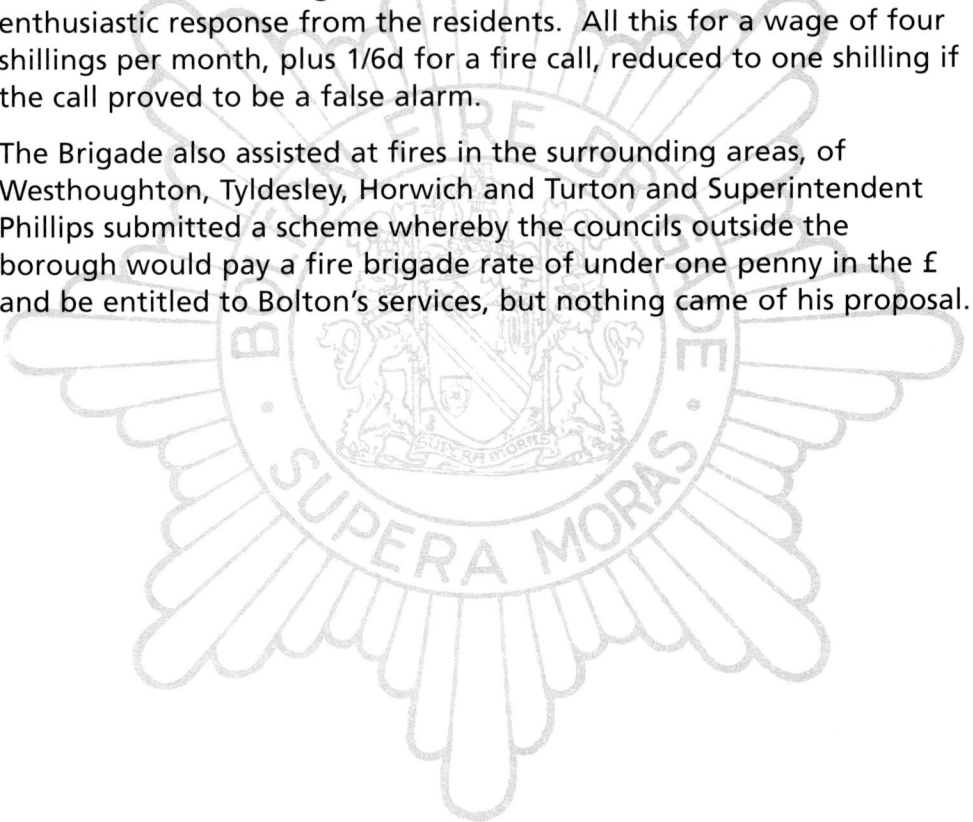

The Egerton Spinning Mill Fire of 1885

On Sunday 17th May 1885 assistance was given at a very serious fire at Egerton. An engineer employed at the Cotton Spinning Mill of Mr. Edmund Ashworth discovered a fire in the third floor spinning room. The Mill, which ran 50,000 to 60,000 spindles, consisted of a seven-storey portion and a new end of three storeys, and was one of a range of buildings, which contained a cotton manufacturing mill and dyeworks.

Following his discovery the engineer immediately raised the alarm and the mill brigade, captained by Mr. William Richardson, promptly turned out, as did Eagley Fire Brigade with its two manual engines "The Deluge" and "Eagle". A force pump driven by 60-foot diameter water wheel, which was normally used to drive a portion of the works, was requisitioned and within 20 minutes copious quantities of water were poured onto the flames. An appeal for assistance went to Bolton and there was a ready response by the town's Brigade with the "Albert" steamer and crew under the command of Deputy Superintendent Kennedy. Superintendent Phillips had been ill for a few weeks but drove up in a cab to render what assistance he could.

Much had happened meanwhile. The fire had a good hold before being discovered and the fifth, sixth, and seventh floors were quickly involved. In well under half an hour a series of crashes announced that the spinning mill roof had disappeared but still the firemen worked determinedly. They were now watched by large crowds that had gathered on the slopes of the surrounding fields. The Mill was doomed – it proved completely impossible to prevent the devastation. There were many stirring sights, not least of which was the burning of the flagstaff on top of the spiral tower and the consuming of the clock, which had long served as the works time keeper. The adjacent threadmill escaped damage but the dyeworks of Mr. Edward Deakin suffered to the extent of several hundred pounds.

The fire loss was estimated at £54,000, a colossal figure for those days. In addition, 300 people were put out of work, which proved to be a tremendous blow for a such a small community.

The Town Centre Fire of 1888

The year 1888 opened with a disastrous town centre fire. At 4.30 am on Wednesday, 4th January, a police constable discovered flames issuing from the roof of the stage area of the Theatre Royal, Churchgate. He immediately contacted the Fire Brigade and within six minutes Supt. Phillips arrived, with two tenders and crews. The Police quickly roused the nearby occupants to evacuate their home. Some houses were already full of smoke and people gathered on Churchgate in their night attire to witness the scene.

Some cattle were rescued from shippens adjoining the rear of the theatre. These shippens were later completely wrecked, with a loss of £700. The theatre roof soon caved in, followed by a series of explosions. As the terrific heat got to the tanks in which the gas for the lime lights was generated, the sky was illuminated for miles, and sparks were carried to the other end of the town.

With help from the police and 20 members of the public, the Brigade got 14 jets to work from Churchgate, Princess Street and Bradshawgate. Supt. Phillips now concentrated on saving the adjoining Star Hotel on one side, and the Victoria Theatre of Varieties on the other. The latter was new and well built and this helped to resist the encroaching fire, although the elaborately furnished refreshment buffet on Churchgate was damaged by fire. Within the hour the theatre was destroyed. An automatic sprinkler system was fitted in the building. Following an investigation, which was carried out by the Police, Superintendent Phillips and the installing engineers, it was found that the sprinkler system had been shut off at the main valve and the leather strap used to lock the valve in the open position had been cut clean through. The manager said he was sure the fire was the work of an incendiary. The fire loss was £1,000.

In a letter to the "Chronicle" newspaper, the manager paid the following tribute to the Brigade – "*They did their duty nobly, fearlessly and well, and it is due to their marvelous exertions that the loss to record is not double what it is, and I only regret that it is not in my power to reward them with something better than words*".

A Fireman's Life in the 1890's

Until 1890, insurance offices and property owners paid for the services of the Brigade but, gradually, theses charges were withdrawn, thus entailing greater expenditure by the corporation. In 1891, after much discussion on the merits and demerits of the attendance of the Brigade to fires outside the Borough, the town council resolved that the Brigade should not attend fires at a greater distance than 2 miles from the Town Hall. This caused the Brigade a lot of anxiety as a result of the difficulties of defining the exact limits of the radius.

During the year, the lot of the firemen started to improve. Prior to this time, apart from seven days annual leave, all their remaining time was either spent at the fire station or on call from their nearby homes. The first improvement was to have a Sunday off every seven weeks. Later this improved to one day off in every four weeks, in addition to their bi-monthly Sunday off. In 1893, when the permanent staff was increased by one, the fire crew additionally got the fifteenth day off. This leave was granted only if it could be done without any inconvenience to the fire department. Pay for a Fireman at this time was £1 6s a week, rising annually to £1 12s per week.

On 26 November, a tragic accident occurred in which auxiliary fireman, Joseph Wilkinson, lost his life. At 5.15 pm, the Brigade was called to a three storey cotton warehouse in Johnson Street. Being near to the fire station, the tender was pushed to the fire. On arrival, flames were issuing from windows and roof. Two jets from hydrants were soon at work. When the flames had been subdued, the job began of clearing the floors of large amounts of smouldering waste.

Willinson, who was a chimney sweep by trade and the oldest of the auxiliaries, was working in dense smoke near the center of the top floor. Five other firemen in the room were busy throwing the cotton down into the yard. Suddenly the floor collapsed taking Wilkinson and two others, along with a large amount of cotton waste, to the floor below. The other three had jumped for the window opening and hung on to the sill. Of the three who had gone through the floor, two escaped with a shaking up, although one of the men was buried up the chest in cotton waste. Fireman Wilkinson could not be seen, although the line of hose that had gone through the floor with him gave his approximate position. Nevertheless, with all the available hands – including police help – clearing away the cotton and rubble, it took over an hour and a half to locate and extricate him. On being found, a doctor pronounced him dead.

The Brigade, unlike the Police at the time, had no permanent local fund to provide for his widow and children, but the Corporation did grant them a small allowance of £15 for the widow and £50 for the children. In 1894 a contributory pension fund was commenced for the permanent staff, and auxiliaries were insured against receiving injuries or being killed on duty.

The most costly fire to occur in Bolton happened on 2 March 1896, at the Rosehill Tannery, Nelson Street, Bolton. The outbreak started at 9.15 pm in the Drying Room of the extensive premises and was first tackled by the Works Fire Brigade. The street fire alarm at Bridgeman Street/Fletcher Street junction was operated at 9.50 pm, and the Borough Brigade turnout, under the command of deputy Superintendent Battern (Superintendent Phillips was incapacitated from injuries received at a fire some weeks before).

On arrival, the Brigade found the premises well alight and in ten minutes the "Albert" and "Foster" steamers were working and, assisted by nearby Mill Brigades, 15 jets were brought to play on the building. The heat was tremendous and much of the surrounding property was endangered. As a precaution, hose lines were run out in all rooms and floors in the nearby mill of Crosses and Dewsbury. All hopes of saving the tannery were abandoned and a tremendous effort was made to save surrounding buildings. By 11 pm the floors collapsed, leaving only a shell. The firemen worked all through the night, working through the ruin of what, the previous day, had been one of the finest tanneries in England. The damage was returned at a colossal figure of £150,000.

The Coronation Street Era Comes to a Close

In 1890 a Sub-Committee was appointed to consider the provision of a new fire station. The Coronation Street Station was considered inadequate for the Brigade, and it was now desirable that living accommodation for the permanent staff should be provided on the station. Various sites were visited and considered inadequate for the Brigade, but it was not until 1896 that it was resolved to build on land at Marsden Road.

The Watch Committee invited architects to submit designs for the new fire station and offered a prize of £50 for the best design, and £25 for the second best. Five designs were submitted and those of Messrs. Cunliffe and Pillins, F.R.I.B.A., were considered best and the design of Mr. W.P. Howarth second best. Tenders for the building were obtained and that of Mr. W. Cunliffe of £12,519 was accepted in September 1897.

As the Coronation Street era drew to a close, the health of Supt. Phillips began to fail. He had received several severe injuries during his service in the brigade. As one who had always led from the front, and this before the advent of breathing apparatus, it meant that he must have taken a lot of punishment whilst fire fighting. After taking sick leave and a holiday to improve his health, he informed the Watch Committee of his resignation by giving one month's notice. Thus ended the career of a man who laid the foundations of the modern Bolton Fire Brigade – a man whose constant endeavour was to increase the efficiency of the Brigade and improve the working conditions of those who served in it. With a handful of full-time men, he had attempted to do the impossible in an age of major industrial fires. On leaving the service, he retired to Southport where he died in 1903.

Deputy Superintendent Mr. Henry Batten was put in charge of the Brigade temporarily and was later given the command, but not before the question of placing the Brigade under Police supervision was discussed. Mr. Batten had led a colourful life. During his youth, son of a sailor, he went to sea when he was ten years old and traveled all over the world – India, Australia, American, Honolulu, Canada and the Antarctic. At the time of the American Civil War he became a blockade-runner but, on the first trip whilst carrying ammunition to the Southerners, his ship was captured by a Northern frigate. The crew were taken to New York as prisoners and strung up by the thumbs for a day. After being released, he made a voyage to Bermuda. Then he joined another blockade-runner, "The Flamingo", running cotton from Galveston. After making three trips, peace was declared. Following a voyage to China, he gave up the sea and joined London Fire Brigade in 1866. He served in London until 1880 when Superintendent Phillips invited him to become engineer of the "Foster" steamer. Thus he became one of the first six of the reorganised Brigade.

In 1898, sets of ladders and equipment were provided and were to be kept at the police stations at Astley Bridge and Middle Hulton for use in case of fire. This did not fully materialize, but some equipment was kept there. This was terminated in 1922.

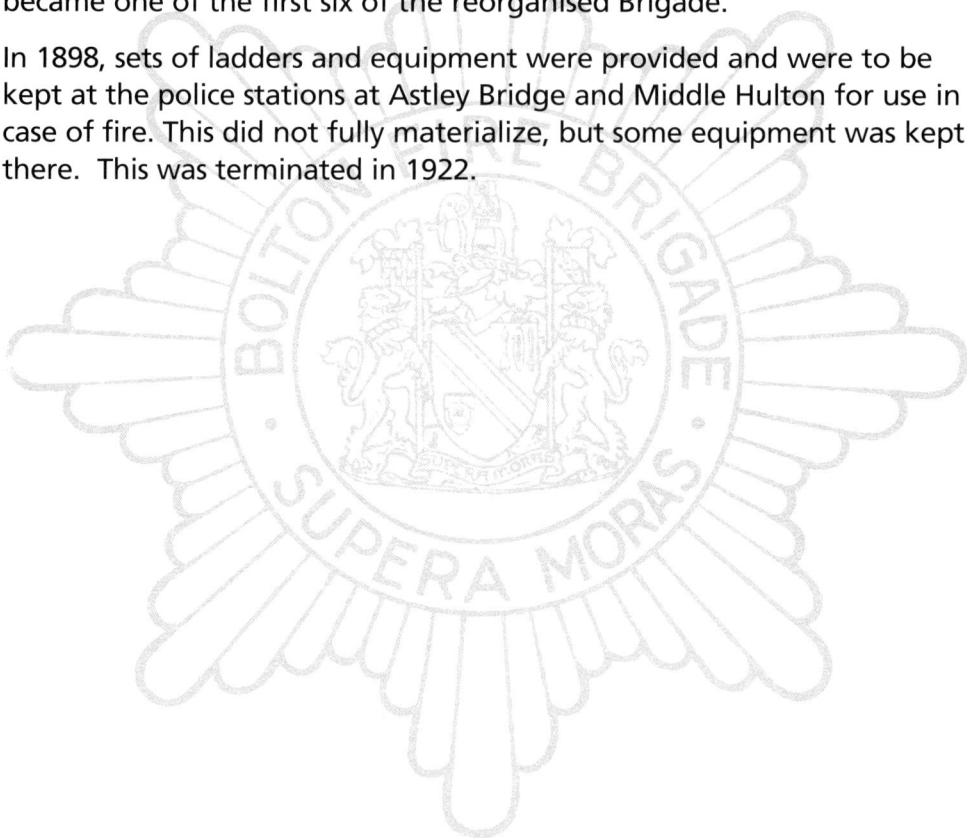

The New Central Fire Station

Bolton's new fire station

1899 saw the opening of the new Central Fire Station at Marsden Road. It was officially opened on 31 October by Councillor Lythgoe, Chairman of the Fire Brigade Sub-Committee. The Mayor, Town Clerk and many members of the Town Council attended the opening ceremony, which was also witnessed by a large crowd that gathered in Marsden Road.

For the first time in Bolton, living accommodation was provided on a Fire Station for the permanent staff and their families. The fact that the firemen now lived on the Station and the locally made "Quick Despatch" harness similar to those used by the New York Fire Brigade at the time – were in use served to cut the turn out time down to about thirty seconds.

Though hailed as one of the finest stations in the country and certainly a tremendous improvement on the Coronation Street

Station, its limitation with regard to the provision of sufficient living accommodation was soon to be felt. A disturbing feature for the new residents was the vibration coming from the huge steam hammer just across the road at the Bolton Forge. These shakings caused gas mantles to break, crockery to fall from shelves, pictures to drop from walls, broken sleep and even necessitated the strengthening of the landing at the rear of the Station. The Engine House had been designed for horse drawn appliances. The potential of the internal combustion engine had not then been realized, resulting, in later years, in very little clearance for petrol and diesel-engined appliances, as they reversed through the narrow doorways into the Engine House.

Besides the opening of the Station, one of the highlights of the proceedings was the showing of the new steamer, officially christened "Victoria" by Councillor Harwood. At this time it was requested that a Code of Rules and Regulations be prepared for the guidance of Fire Brigade men. Also, at this time underground tanks were built in the Town Hall Square - these were tested by the steamers "Foster" and "Victoria". The tank on the north side is still there to this day and was used with good effect in the Town Hall fire in 1981

Bolton Fire Brigade
in the 20th Century

In 1900, Bolton Fire Brigade Sub-Committee was trying to evaluate pumps, appliances and equipment, as only the best would do for Bolton. As a result two members of the committee were sent, as delegates, to the International Congress in Berlin in July and, also, to visit Hamburg to check their conditions and appliances and report back how the rest of Britain and Europe were dealing with Fire Brigade developments. What follows are a number of reports on these visits which were subsequently presented to the Fire Brigade Sub-Committee and provide some interesting insights into fire service developments nationally and internationally during this period..

Congress Report 1 – Hamburg Visit

Gentlemen,

Acting upon the resolution adopted by the Committee upon the 14th April last, instructing us to visit Hamburg to inspect appliances there, and appointing us as delegates to the International Congress, at Berlin, we left Bolton on 3rd June and proceeded direct from London to Hamburg, arriving early on Wednesday, 5th June.

We had an appointment at 10 am at the Central Fire Station in Stitaler Strasse, and were courteously received by the Second Officer – the Brand Direcktor, Herr Westphalien, having previously advised us of his compulsory absence in Berlin, as Chairman of the Congress Committee.

One of the Brandmeisters (Superintendent) showed us through the Central Station and gave us a practical exhibition of many of their appliances. Afterwards, we were driven to No. 10 Station, a large new Sub-Station, about two miles from the center of the city.

At the Central Station, we saw one of the Shand Mason steamer fire engines, which they had purchased, as a model. And had several built by local makers on the same principal. We were very much impressed by seeing, for the first time, what our Committee have long felt to be desirable – several combination, carbonic acid gas engines and ladder escapes. The Hamburg Brigade possesses nine such vehicles built specially on the design of the Brand Direcktor, on a model of one first purchased from Messrs. Magirus Ulm. The cost was about £279 each, and each weighs, with all equipment on, about three and a half tons. In our opinion, the vehicles are unnecessarily heavy and could be built much lighter. Each machine carries a large tank capable of carrying about one hundred gallons of water. Two large cylinders of liquefied carbonic acid gas were also carried, these being sufficient for four hundred gallons of water. Also, large hose reels with a 3/8 nozzle. Another nozzle was shown to us, which could be regulated into four sizes of delivery through a cone. We were also shown a patent smoke helmet, supplied with fresh air from the combined machine by means of a small air pump driven by the compressed carbonic acid gas.

We also saw in operation, a patent suit and helmet to be used in case of a severe conflagration. An arrangement at the top of the helmet allowed the wearer to turn on, at will, water from the mains, whereby a douche completely covered him and afforded protection in a very severe fire. This, to our mind, was not of much utility, as a fire so fierce as to necessitate the use of such apparatus, would render the building unsafe to enter.

The Hamburg Brigade consists of ten stations (including the Central). At each Station there are six Foremen, four Drivers and twenty two Firemen and, in addition at the Central, on Brand Direcktor, one Brand Inspector and three Brand Meisters, making a total staff of three hundred and twenty five. In addition to this, a large number of workmen and six clerks are employed at the Central Station.

There are twelve steam Fire Engines of 250 gpm, five of 450 gpm, eleven of 750 gpm. The number of other vehicles (beyond the nine combination machines mentioned) we were unable to accurately ascertain, but at each Station there is a large store wagon fitted out with all requisites for dealing with serious fires.

Portable electric lamps, accumulator charged, are carried on all vehicles, and will last six hours. All stores in bulk, also clothing for men, are kept at Central Station.

In quick turn outs, we are ahead of anything we saw – the quickest being 25 seconds – whereas we regularly turn out in less than half that time.

The population of Hamburg is 780,000; the annual cost of the Fire Brigade is £88,000. We should state that all plans for new buildings in the city have to be submitted to the Headquarters of the Fire Brigade, and all new buildings are inspected by Brigade staff - all this in 1901.

Congress Report 2 – Berlin Visit

On arrival, we found the arrangements for the convenience of foreign delegates were very imperfect. Matters appeared by have been delayed and no interpreters were provided for any foreign representatives.

Upon obtaining our German credentials, we attended the Congress, which was held at The Reichstag (the German Imperial Houses of Parliament). The Congress was attended by over 1500 delegates from also every nation in Europe, also by representatives from America and Canada.

One paper was read by Mr. E.C. Sachs of London, Chairman of the British Fire Prevention Committee. Mr. Gamble, Second Officer of the Metropolitan Fire Brigade also spoke.

The Congress itself, although apparently hearty and enthusiastic, was practically no use to us, as all papers and most of the speeches were given in the German language.

In the afternoon we were shown through the very extensive works of the Berlin Electricity Company. All machinery was driven by electrical power and was on a most modern principle. In the evening we attended the banquet held in the International Fire Exhibition Building. The same was very well attended by the foreign representatives and each nation was voiced by one of the delegates. Major Fox of The London Salvage Corps. Speaking for the English section.

On Friday morning we again visited the exhibition, which is about three miles from the center of the city. About £21,000 had been spent on the erection of buildings and the exhibition had been opened, by the Empress, on the Saturday previous to our visit.

To those interested in Fire Brigade work, the exhibition was an unqualified success and is admitted to be the best of its kind ever held. Every conceivable appliance connected with our Department appeared to be shown - the exhibitors being from all parts of the continent, and America, Germany and Austria perhaps predominant. There were no exhibits from England.

We paid three visits to the Exhibition it being impossible to inspect all in one day. We found that, although not represented at Congress, Birmingham and Liverpool had specially sent their Superintendents to the exhibition. We saw the Pneumatic Steel Telescope Ladder Escape (makers W.C.F. Dusch of Frankfurt) in operation, which gained the Grand Prix at Paris last year. However, the weight, together with the cost and want of a combination, did not commend itself as suitable for Bolton.

We saw many very interesting exhibits, of which – not being practical to us – it would be useless to particularize. However, we would mention a small Benzine Motor Engine (Maker Magerius Ulm), which we saw working. It appeared to be a very handy machine and suitable for small fires.

There were a large number of Ladder Escapes, also Carbonic Acid Gas Engines and Ladder Escapes combined, such as we have previously had under consideration. The two we though best were: -

No. 1 made in Brenner – this machine carried two tanks, each capable of holding about 120 gallons of water, also two hose reels and an attachable truck behind for ordinary canvas hose. The ladders on this machine were portable. It would require continuous drill for our own men to be expert in the use of same. The weight of the vehicle is about 45 cwts.

No. 2 vehicle is made in Vienna – the construction of this machine is similar to No. 2 but, instead of portable ladders, carries a trussed ladder escape. Its weight is about 3 tons and the cost was stated to be about £290 - £300. We have since requested the Town Clerk to write for further particulars and, definitely, as to price as, although we paid three visits we could not find a reliable person in charge who could supply us with the information required.

We have now ascertained that the Brenner was made by the staff of Brenner Brigade whilst the Vienna Engine was made for the Vienna Fire Brigade by Mr W. Knaust of Vienna who letter and catalogue is now submitted. The three principal makers of the combined engine and escape are at Frankfurt, Ulm and Vienna.

We are now more strongly confirmed in the opinion held by the members of our committee that we should possess some such vehicle as referred to (No. 1 and No.2) for the first turn out to fires, and if replies are not satisfactory, we would recommend such being built, either locally or by English makers to our design.

During the afternoon of Friday we witnessed a fine display of practice at the headquarters of Berlin Fire Brigade. Over three hundred firemen took part in same. There was a very fine exhibition of drill and in the sham fire ten vehicles and one steamer took part. At Hamburg and Berlin, at the central stations (where the men receive their training) there is erected a large model of a large warehouse (sketch submitted) and the men were thoroughly drilled in scaling a life saving. A rough model of the exterior of a cotton mill would doubtless be very useful at our own station. Several novel appliances were used in ladder drills.

Attached to a strong leather belt worn by each Fireman, is a strong steel Snap which is used for attachment to the ladder staves, thus enabling the Firemen to have free use of both hands when in an elevated position. Each Fireman also carries a small reel of line and pulley, which enables him to establish communications from his position and the ground.

The portable light ladders are ingeniously arranged with strong iron clutches for insertion in windows and, by these means, the scaling is comparatively easy. Hook belts and hook ladders – we took the liberty of ordering one belt, together with one iron clutch for the top of the ladder and, if approved, no doubt these can be made locally. The preserving snaps appear to be almost an absolute necessity, and ought to be supplied to every fireman.

On Friday evening we attended a fete at the Zoological Gardens in the Thiergarten, and on Saturday night were entertained by the Mayor and Aldermen in the Rathaus (Guildhall). Representatives from all European nations were present and the entertainment was unique and enjoyable.

Our visit has confirmed our opinion as to the utility of chemical engines and, at the same time, proved that it is unnecessary for chemical engines and ladder escapes to be separate vehicles. Thus necessitating two turn outs at each fire as at Liverpool, Leeds

Congress Report 3 – London Visit

In accordance with our appointment by the Watch Committee on the 11th March 1903, and confirmed by the Council on the 1st April 1903, we visited London to attend the International Fire Prevention Congress held at Caxton Hall, Westminster, in connection with the Fire Exhibition at Earls Court.

The Congress was opened by the Lord Mayor of London on Monday morning, 6th July, at 11 am, before a brilliant assemblage, and was closed on Thursday evening, 9th July, by a Conversazione on the invitation of the Directors of the Exhibition at Earls Court.

Fifteen different foreign and colonial peoples were represented at the Congress, which was attended by over 700 members and, in our opinion, it has been a great success from an international and educational point of view. We think that the bringing together of so many nationalities for the interchange of ideas, the recording of experiences and discussion of the best means of combating that dreadful foe, a constant terror to communities all over the world, is worthy of encouragement and support.

We were very pleased with arrangements made by the Fire Prevention Committee of Great Britain to bring before Congress, the important subjects – first, the best means of preventing fire and, second, the best means of extinguishing it. We think that the untiring efforts of Mr. Sachs, the Chairman of the Committee, and Mr. Marsland, the Honourary Secretary, and their assistants, in organizing the Congress and arrangements for the comfort of those who attended it, are deserving of the highest praise.

The opening ceremony, presided over by the Lord Mayor of London, was attended and addressed by representatives of the British Government and very interesting speeches were delivered by the French Prefect of Police of Paris, Monsieur Lepine, by the special Delegate sent by the Czar of Russia, Prince Alexander Lvoff, and by Delegates from Germany, Austria, Italy, Belgium, United States of America and Australia. During the Congress, 38 Papers were read and discussions held on various subjects connected with the prevention or extinguishments of fire.

One of the most interesting we heard being given by Guy Pym, Esq. M.P., on the necessity of placing Fire Brigades on a legal basis in which he urged the necessity of uniformity in efficiency in equipment and even in clothing. He also strongly advocated that local authorities should be compelled, by Act of Parliament, to equip and maintain, under Government inspection, adequate appliances for the protection from fire of property in their district and under their control. The listening of this paper and the discussion which followed led us to consider whether, in the opinion of experts expressed at this meeting, our own town would come up to the standard of being adequately equipped if such an Act of Parliament were to be passed, and our Fire Brigade were to be placed under Government inspection.

We feel bound to admit and to report to you that we think Bolton is neither adequately equipped nor sufficiently manned if we take into account the many very large and valuable properties existing within its limits which would, in the event of one large fire occurring, would be totally without protection by the communal authorities.

We venture to suggest that such a state of things ought not to be allowed to continue and to point out that the member of the Watch and its Sub-Committee, which looks after the interests of the Fire Brigade, are taking upon themselves a very serious responsibility and are laying themselves open to a grave charge of neglect in delaying the complete furnishing of the splendid fire station which has been erected to so great an expense.

We do not wish to enter into details of the incompleteness of our appliances, but we are confident that something should be done at once to bring our fire station up to date, and recommend that a fire escape and chemical engine combined, such as the one we submit a tracing and photograph, should be purchased immediately. It is made and has been supplied by Messrs. Merryweather & Co. to several towns, some much smaller than Bolton, and we are satisfied it is the best one on the market at the present time. The price is about £300.

We also recommend that an estimate should be got in for a new steam fire engine to replace the one which, at present, appears ornamenting our new fire station, but it is quite worthless and obsolete and is not fit to take out for practical use. Taking into consideration the little accommodation we have for stabling, we suggest that, in lieu of the horses, the new fire engine should be propelled by a motor in combination similar to the one lately acquired by Liverpool and several other towns – one of which we saw at the exhibition and which ought to be seen by the committee and enquired about before an order for another engine is given.

Before closing this report, we beg to thank the Watch Committee for having given us the opportunity of attending the Congress and visiting the exhibition.

Signed: D. Maginnis   W.H. Brown

Fire Brigade Developments in the Early 1900s

In 1903, permission was granted to alter the new fire station to accommodate six single men's quarters and extra stabling. The new combination chemical engine was purchased from Messrs. Merryweather for £347.00. The old manual (1870) was refurbished by Brigade personnel and sold to Gillingham District Fire Brigade for £25. Also, the "Albert" steam engine (1868) that was worn out was sold back the makers for £40.

First pump and crew, 1905.

In 1905, in March, a new steam fire engine arrived and named "Alexandra" (after the Queen) was examined and tested on Victoria Square before the Watch Committee – cost £284. The suggested motor propulsion did not materialize and the Brigade remained horse drawn.

Superintendent Batten retired in 1905 and his deputy, Mr. John Jones, was appointed. Supt. Jones joined Bolton in 1882, having previously served in Salford and Manchester. He did much to encourage local works fire brigades and was a keen supporter of the Lancashire Fire Brigade's Friendly Society. Due to the Brigade's connection with ambulance work he was in demand as a Lecturer in First Aid. He was made an Honourary Scoutmaster for his services to that movement.

Superintendent Jones, mindful of the monotony of a fireman's life brought about by constant attendance at the station, arranged for speakers to visit the station and lecture on various subjects. Concert parties and billiard matches were also arranged, and an application was made to the Libraries' Committee to borrow 30 books per month for the use of the firemen. All was greatly appreciated by the men and their families.

Staff at Bolton Fire Station, 1906.

View of fireman and combination chemical engine 1903, carried escape and gas tanks for hose reels.

The steamer Alexandra and crew.

In 1908, the Town Clerk reported that the total expenditure incurred by them for the new fire station in Marsden Road had amounted to £17,079, and the borrowing power for that purpose under the Bolton Improvement Act 1897, amounted to £14,600, showing a sum of £2,480 to have been expended on the capital account over and above the authorised borrowing power. In order to cover such excess expenditure it is desirable than application should be made to the local Government Board for their approval of a further borrowing of £2,480. In November 2000, as I write, Marsden Road Fire Station is being demolished to make way for town centre improvements, at a total cost of £60,000.

The stables 1907-8. My maternal grandfather and uncle:
Edward Farrell and son, John Edward Farrell.

In 1910, he again raised the question of the purchase of a motor
pump but the appliances, again, remained horse-drawn. Riding a
horse-drawn tender at full gallop could prove a hair-raising
experience – sometimes not without mishap. One fireman suffered a
double fracture to the left leg when he was flung off the tender as
its wheels stuck in the tram line at Deansgate/Bradshawgate junction.

In 1911, the request for improvement of rest day was granted – one
day off in eight. In the same year Superintendent Jones retired but,
regrettably, his retirement was short as he died in June 1912.
The post was advertised at £150 per year, plus uniform, house,
coal and gas free. From 58 applicants, a short list of 6 was selected
and, of these, the man chosen was Mr. Herbert Bentley, an Inspector
of Police and Chief Officer of the South Shields Fire Brigade,
who had also served at Bradford, his native city.

Staff at Bolton Fire Station, 1912.
Back row: 1st left Fm Sykes, 1st right Fm Edward Farrell, 2nd row 5th right; JC Treacher, 6th right Superintendant Herbert Bentley, 2nd row 1st left Fm R Bailey, 1st right Fm Edward Conway.

Fire rig 1900s
Fm Edward Conway

Mr. Bentley took up the case for motorisation and, in January 1913, it was resolved to purchase a motor ambulance and, in April, another resolution to purchase a motor fire engine with a 500 gallon per minute pump. An Austin ambulance was delivered in May. The first motor fire engine, a Leyland, at a cost of £1000, was delivered in December 1913, and a second one was ordered for the following March but, due to Leyland Motors being on war work, delivery did not take place until early 1916.

Bolton's first motor fire engine, 1913.

The War Years - National Emergency

In May 1914 a letter was received and read to the Fire Brigade committee from Remount Office, Bowerham Barrack, Lancaster, intimating that it is lawful for the State, on declaration of an emergency by His Majesty, to impress such horses and vehicles as are required by the military forces, and stating that horses and vehicles belonging to this Committee Fire Department had been inspected and that it was probable that, in the event of an emergency, the horses detailed communication would be required if still in the committee's possession, and that the same would be purchased at a fair valuation.

Bolton's bomb damage, September 1915 after Zepplin air raid.

Bolton's bomb damage, September 1915 after Zepplin air raid.

On arrival they were confronted with several serious fires and repeated explosions as the fire reached stocks of live shells. The factory covered an area of about two square miles. The employees had been withdrawn, and the water main feeding the site had been put out of action by an explosion. There was a general lack of direction, and the initiative was left to the assisting Brigades. Ultimately, water was relayed from a dyke, via pumps, from Liverpool, Salford, and Manchester Brigades into a canvas dam directly on to the fire. The crews had been warned to take cover, but the buildings that would have provided cover had all been flattened by explosions, so the firemen had to repeatedly drop to the ground as shells exploding in all directions spent themselves. The water mains were put back in commission the following day. This allowed the assisting Brigades to be withdrawn and Bolton pump returned to station, having been away twenty-seven hours.

The Town Clerk received a telegram from Mr. Winston Churchill (then Minister of Munitions) expressing appreciation of the high qualities of energy, courage and endurance displayed by the detachment in face of danger resulting from frequent explosions, and great gratification of the successful results of their efforts, which were instrumental in saving a large portion of the factory from destruction. On 3rd December 1918 at the Town Hall, Lancaster, Superintendent Brocklehurst and several officers from other Lancashire Brigades that had attended the Morecambe fire, were presented with The King's Police Medal by Lord Shuttleworth, Lord Lieutenant of Lancashire. Of the firemen who served with the Forces during the war, Ernest Townsend died in Egypt, Edward McGowan was killed in action, and auxiliary fireman, John Riley (Military Medal) died after being invalided out suffering from gas poisoning.

April 1917, saw the sale of the Bolton horse-drawn appliances – one horse drawn ambulance, one horse-drawn first aid chemical engine, and two horse-drawn hose tenders. Thus, after many years, the Brigade became completely motorized.

On standby: 14 days on, one day off.

Cotton mill fires were still prevalent and always hazardous. At a fire in a mill in St. Johns Street, in December 1919, a crew was working at a fire on the top floor when the roof fell in, trapping one of them in the middle of the floor. The remainder of the crew, including the Deputy Superintendent although suffering badly from the effects of smoke, managed to stagger down into the yard, where two of them collapsed. The trapped man, now surrounded by fire, managed to get to a window and called for help. The crew got a ladder to the Boiler House roof and an employee, James Mann, attempted to throw a line from the roof to the window. This was unsuccessful and so he climbed a downspout to a height of about 40 feet and got the line to the fireman. The fireman tied the line to a spinning mule carriage and climbed down to the boiler house roof. On reaching ground level, he was taken to hospital suffering from burns to his face and hands. Later, in recognition of his action, James Mann was presented with the Bronze Medal of the Society for the Protection of Life from Fire.

The Roaring '20's and '30's

1920, saw a change of title from that of Superintendent of the Brigade to that of Chief Fire Officer. Several surrounding councils made enquiries regarding Bolton making provision for fire cover in their district and, in 1923, an agreement, initially for five years, was made with Turton Urban District Council. The effect of this was to double the Brigade turn out area. Over fifty square miles of territory, ranging from the industrially concentrated town to the sparsely populated out district, which contained 237 working farms, was covered by Marsden Road Station. Bolton has provided this service continuously since that year.

Service funeral of chief officer Bentley's son 1926

Another change of resignation of rank occurred in 1927 – the rank of Engineer was re-designated to that of Sub-Officer.

As the design of fire engines developed, consideration was given to the purchase of a turntable ladder. In 1928, delivery was taken of an 85 ft. Leyland-Metz ladder, which could be used for rescue purposes or as a water tower onto upper floors of blazing buildings.

The original Leyland appliances were due for replacement. Further Leylands were purchased – one in 1934 with a Braidwood body, and one in 1936 with a limousine body. These machines were powered with by 50 horse power engines, had complexly separate duel ignition (magneto and coil) systems, and pumping units each capable of delivery 750 gallons per minute. One disquieting feature in their design was a 25 gallons capacity feed petrol tank sited in front of the officers' knees within the driving cab!

On the 14th May 1935, there occurred a fatal accident, involving fireman Arthur Winterburn. Whilst responding to a fire call in Newport Street on an open appliance, Winterburn overbalanced and fell off as the engine turned into Victoria Square. He suffered serious head injuries from which he died early the following day. He was 28 years of age with very good prospects in the service.

Emergency telephones (Ericcson Pillars) for Police use, but also in contact with the Fire Brigade and Ambulance Services, had been sited throughout the Borough, therefore, there was no necessity for the Street Fire Alarm System and it was dismantled in 1936.

By this time, hours of duty had been reduced to three days continuous duty, with the fourth day off. Due to the living quarters at the station being full to capacity, there was little prospect of the younger married firemen getting married quarters for several years. Following a discussion of the problems, a Special Sub-Committee examined the following alternatives –

1. To provide housing adjacent to the fire station

2. Extend the existing fire station

3. Erect a fire station on an entirely new site

Before any action was taken on the above proposals, an event took place, which altered the situation. The Secretary of the Fire Brigade Union wrote to the Town Clerk asking that the Council be approached with a view to ending the continuous duty system, by the introduction of a two-shift system. In addition to the above, long discussions took place with a representative of the Home Office with a view to providing extra accommodation for additional appliances and men, under a scheme as a safeguard against the risk of possible incendiary attack from the air.

The outcome was that the Brigade recruited 22 additional men and the two-shift (two platoon) system came into operation on the 9th September 1937. This allowed the men not on duty to go to their own homes, although they were expected to attend the station if requested. The need for auxiliaries was eliminated by this move, thus the Brigade was now staffed entirely by full-time personnel.

The 1937 Factories' Act imposed a duty on the local authorities to inspect certain factories, with a view to certifying that they were provided with satisfactory means of escape in case of fire.
The responsibility was delegated to the Brigade and, as a result of this, 11 of the personnel were authorised to carry out the inspections. Alterations to the station were commenced and a drill ground was provided, with a view to training the new auxiliaries who were to be recruited under the emergency Fire Brigade organisation.

Throughout this period, the Auxiliary Fire Service (AFS) expanded rapidly, particularly before and after the outbreak of war. So that, by the end of 1940, in addition to the whole time Brigade, there were 297 full-time and 811 part-time AFS personnel based on the main Station, and 11 sub-stations. These sub-stations had been requisitioned for the emergency and many were little more than garages to house 67 vehicles, 27 large trailer pumps, 78 light trailer pumps, and some 66,000 feet of hose and equipment that had been issued to the local AFS.

The Second World War

During the war, assistance was sought by cities suffering from the worst effects of the air raid blitz in Manchester and Liverpool. On 7th May, a contingency some 79 strong with appliances and equipment drawn from Bolton and District, left for Liverpool with Sub-Officer P. Catterall (a whole-time member of the Bolton Fire Brigade) in charge.

On arrival, the party was dispersed to various major incidents. The Sub-Officer, along with auxiliary firemen, E. Hitchon, S. Emmason, G. Longmate, and J. Isherwood, were employed at large fires in warehouse premises. Just before midnight, an air raid siren sounded the alert and, within minutes, the blitz had started again. Incendiaries and high explosive bombs showered down on the area. Isherwood was killed outright in the street. Emmason, who was in charge of a trailer pump, ran to help as a nearby air raid shelter containing civilians and a soldier, received a direct hit. Though badly shaken and despite further falling bombs, he succeeded in extricating the soldier who was seriously injured and dragged him 300 yds. to the canal bank. He then lost consciousness and was later found by a search party. Hitchon, who had been burned by an oil bomb, along with others, was receiving first aid from Longmate in a shelter when that too was hit. Both of them assisted in rescuing the other occupants of the shelter when another near miss buried Hitchon in the wreckage of the shelter – he died shortly afterwards.

As a result of their actions during the operation, Acting Sub-Officer Catterall received the British Empire Medal, Auxiliary Firemen Emmason, Longmate and Hitchon (posthumously) received commendation in the London Gazette.

The task of effectively running the Auxilary Fire Service, alongside some 1,000 Independent Fire Authorities, was becoming increasingly difficult and, following high level discussions, the Home Secretary announced that the service would be nationalised. As a result of this, on the 18th August 1941, all Fire Authorities were dissolved and the National Fire Service (NFS) was born.

Prior to this date, Bolton Chief Mr. H. Blackledge, had been appointed Area Fire Force Commander and, in the short period before nationalization became effective, Third Officer, R.C. Bentley – son of Mr. Herbert Bentley, a former Chief, was appointed temporary Chief Officer.

The Manchester fire boats with some of the crew from Bolton 1940's

'Happy hour' at Bolton fire station believed to be 1st may 1940. The night of the Manchester Blitz. Dickie Henderson and twins plus company from the grand theatre. Most of the fire crews are from Newcastle area on standby.

During the NFS years, some Bolton firemen were detached or posted to Liverpool and Manchester and worked throughout the blitz on fire boats (converted canal barges) carrying extra heavy pumps and worked at many larges fires along Manchester city canals. Additionally, there were two further casualties amongst the Bolton personnel in the war years. Column Officer P. Bradshaw, a former whole-time member of the Bolton Brigade, and fireman Bradburn, were both killed in separate accidents whilst responding to emergency calls.

AFS and NFS crews in training and manning appliances 1940

AFS and NFS crews in training and manning appliances 1940

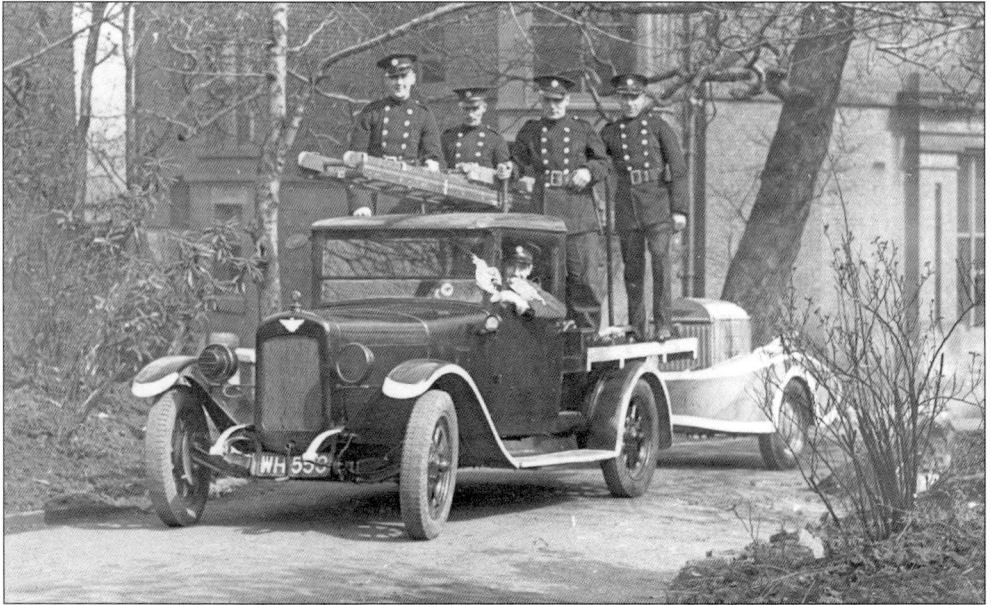

AFS and NFS crews in training and manning appliances 1940

1943 Bolton's new turntable ladder

The national fire service staff at Burnthwaite 1942

Junior officers training at Brighton 1946

The Post War Years

Following the war, the National Fire Service, as promised by the Home Secretary, was disbanded and Bolton regained its Brigade on 1st April 1948. Brigades were now formed under the authority of the Fire Services Act 1947. An Act which was to ensure an efficient service nationally and prevent any repetition of the near chaotic pre-war days.

A Government grant was paid towards the cost of providing the service and the Home Office saw that standards were maintained by regular inspections of the Brigades.

On the de-nationalisation of the service, the former Chief, Mr. H. Blackledge, was appointed Chief Officer of the newly formed Lancashire County Fire Brigade, and the Bolton post went to Mr. R.C. Bentley.

The numerical strength of the Brigade was now almost double the pre-war figure, and the service - whose prestige had been enhanced by its excellent war record – recruited many de-mobbed personnel from the Armed Forces who maintained high standards of discipline and morale. The post-war Brigade carried on the war-time tradition of employing firewomen. Thus the control room was staffed by eight of them who worked in pairs to give round the clock cover.

The first major advance in the re-formed Brigade was the introduction of mobile radio. The Police controlled the main station and the Fire Brigade shared the air via a sub-control when they were attending emergency calls. The radio proved to be a boon to the service. Calls could now be re-checked and additional information given en-route to emergences. Urgent assistance or stop messages could now be sent back to the control much more quickly. Prior to the installation of the radio, a member of the fire crew (usually the youngest or the most fleet of foot) would dash off clutching a hastily scribbled "Stop" message and two pennies in the hope of finding a telephone within a reasonable distance. Sometimes this proved no mean feat in a sparsely populated area in the dead of night!

Call out at Bolton fire station

Bolton fire station control room

Vernon Humpage Ltd, Bradshawgate 1950

Deep lift tests for new pump ladder XWH700

On parade, 1950s. Left to right: H Hampson, T. Regan, A. Veevers, S. Stonehewer, H. Bradshaw, T. Haslam, B. Rimmer, F. Watson, V. Short, R. Bradshaw, J. Pritchard, J. Pilkington and N. Hilton.

Friday routines 1950s

Control room 1950

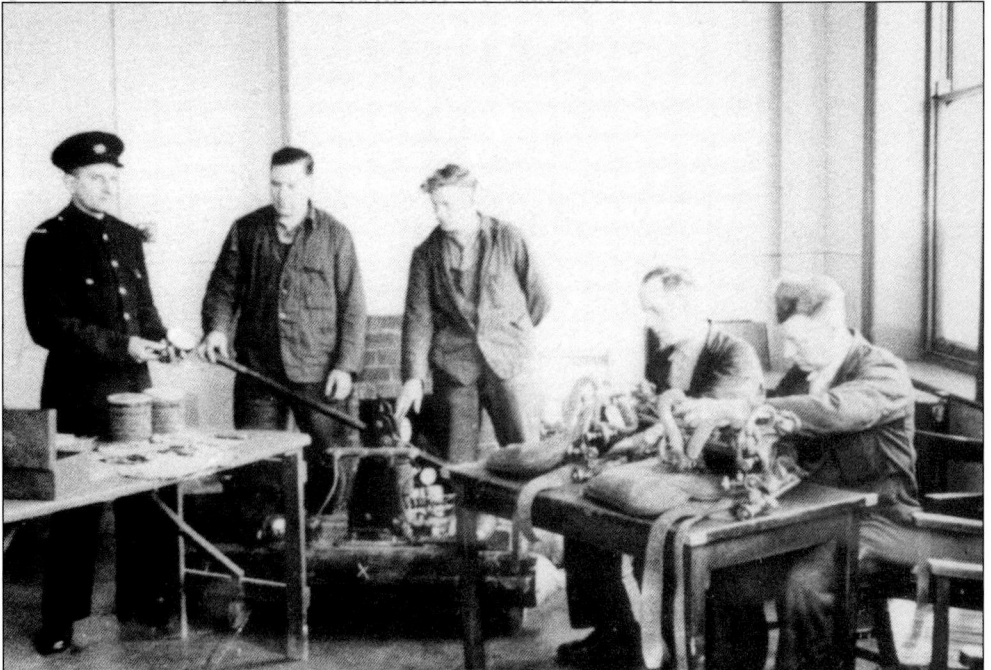

Breathing apparatus training

AFS Training

Daily checks

Output tests

Drill

The replacement of war-time appliances commenced with the purchase of two petrol- engined comers – one for use as a water tender, the other a salvage tender. The latter was destined to give excellence service at cotton mill fires, which were a predominant feature of the Brigade's work in the immediate post-war years. The diesel-engined, "Merryweather" pump escape was purchased in 1951. This heralded the gradual change over to diesel-engined front line appliances, which was to take place over the years.

Appliance room Marsden Road, 1951

Petrol tanker and garage fire, Knowles Garage, Astley Bridge 1951

Full house, Christmas 1951

Metal powder explosion and fire 1951

Home Office inspection, 1951

AFS training

The cold war of the post-war years made it necessary to re-establish the Civil Defence and the Auxiliary Fire Service was reformed. However, recruitment was very disappointing as very few persons volunteered their services. One feature in the modern service has been the increasing readiness on the part of the public to call the Brigade to emergencies other than fires. Thus they attend a very wide variety of calls, ranging from animals in distress, the removal of gale-damaged structures, the release of persons trapped in crashed vehicles, persons stuck in lifts or locked out of their homes, pumping out flooded homes and cellars, attending spillages of flammable liquids and corrosive chemicals.

Fire at Levers Rope Walk, 1952

Fire at Whitehouse Roxalina Street, 1952

Fire Watersmeeting Bleach Works 1952

Ready for exercise at Liverpool 1952

RSPCA Shearlegs rescue training 1952

Appliances ready for HQ Inspection 1953

Life saving class 1953

AFS exercise 1953

AFS exercise 1953

Home Office drill 1953

*Fire and explosion, Lum Street
Gas Works 1954*

Smithills Hall Show 1954

The Brigade gave valuable assistance at two major local incidents that occurred in 1954 and 1957. The first of these happened on 21st May 1954 –

Special service call Corporation Street, Bolton, May 1954

a three-storey shop in Corporation Street was undergoing structural alterations but was still open for business. Shortly after lunch time, a main supporting pillar collapsed and the entire frontage fell into, a normally very busy street. A woman on an upper floor waiting to try on a dress was hurled into the street below and a second, who was passing at the time, was buried in the debris. Fortunately, both survived the accident. The Brigade rescued seven assistants trapped on the upper floors and, assisted by members of the Defence Corps., made a thorough search of the rubble. Also, oxyacetylene equipment was used from the head of the turntable ladder to cut away a girder hanging dangerously from the roof.

HO inspection 1954

HO inspection 1954

Royal visit 1954

Special service call 1955

AFS training

Training for civil defence 1954-55

Training for civil defence 1954-55

Fire at Temple Bleach Works 1956

Fire at Vantona Textiles 1957

Fire at Bell Cinema, June 1957

RADIAC exercise, AFS 1957

Drill 1957

Control room 1957

HO Inspection, 1957

HO Inspection, 1957

The second incident occurred on the 12th September 1957, about 7 am, when a resident of Fylde Street, Moses Gate, noticed a crack in the road and called the Police. Shortly afterwards, walls began to crack and pavements crumbled. The Police evacuated the immediate area and, by 11 am, the road had entirely caved in, taking 11 houses with it. The main sewer had collapsed creating a huge cavity under the road and adjoining properties. By 7 pm, 16 houses had partially collapsed. More than 100 nearby homes had been evacuated – thus making 400 people temporarily homeless.

Special service call, Fylde Street sewer collapse, September 1957

Special service call, Fylde Street sewer collapse, September 1957

Fylde Street is on the boundary between Bolton and Farnworth and fire crews from Bolton and Lancashire County Fire Brigade were quickly on the scene. Initially, all domestic fires and naked lights were extinguished to prevent possible explosions from leaking gas mains. Several pumps were set into the craters and into sewer inspection pits further back from the disaster area, in an attempt to divert sewage and rainwater, but torrential rain stretched 18 pumps to the limit, and three 6" plastic pipes lines laid by the Brigade were working at maximum capacity for several days. In all one mile of pipeline was used.

Many families carried furniture and personal possessions away from the stricken area and nearby friends and neighbours rallied wonderfully by taking in families or storing goods. Brigade pumps had to be used intermittently until 9th October, and, although the incident was only two miles from the Station, Bolton appliances clocked over 1,300 miles in transporting relief crews, fuel supplies, hoses and the like. 3,500 man hours were put in by Bolton Fire Brigade before the incident was closed.

Special service call, carboy off lorry, 1957

Back from a job, 1957. SubO R Prosser, Fm S. Brookes, Fm T. Gregson, Fm T. Self.

In 1958, Bolton Fire Brigade and Lancashire County Fire Brigade were involved in a search and rescue operation when a civilian airplane crashed into the side of Winter Hill. Thirty-five people were killed.

Fire at Barlow and Jones, Blackburn Road, June 1958

Fire, Temple Works, February 1959

The sights of the 1960's

Pump escape crew, 1960.
H. Bradshaw, J. Lever, W. Holt, J. Pilkington, J. Liptrot.

Pump ladder, C. Hobbs, T. Grundy, B. Rimmer, A. Smith, A. Hilton.

Salvage tender, R. Bradshaw, J. Liptrot, R. Nightingale, L. Ward.

Drill. L. Ward, B. Harrison, W. Stallard.

AFS training with new green goddesses 1960

Inside of cotton mill showing mule spinning room, 1960

Henry Stratton warehouse, 1960

On the night of 1st May 1961, there occurred the worst fire in the history of the Brigade, in terms of numbers of lives lost. The disaster, which received world wide publicity, happened at the Top Storey Club, Crown Street, Bolton.

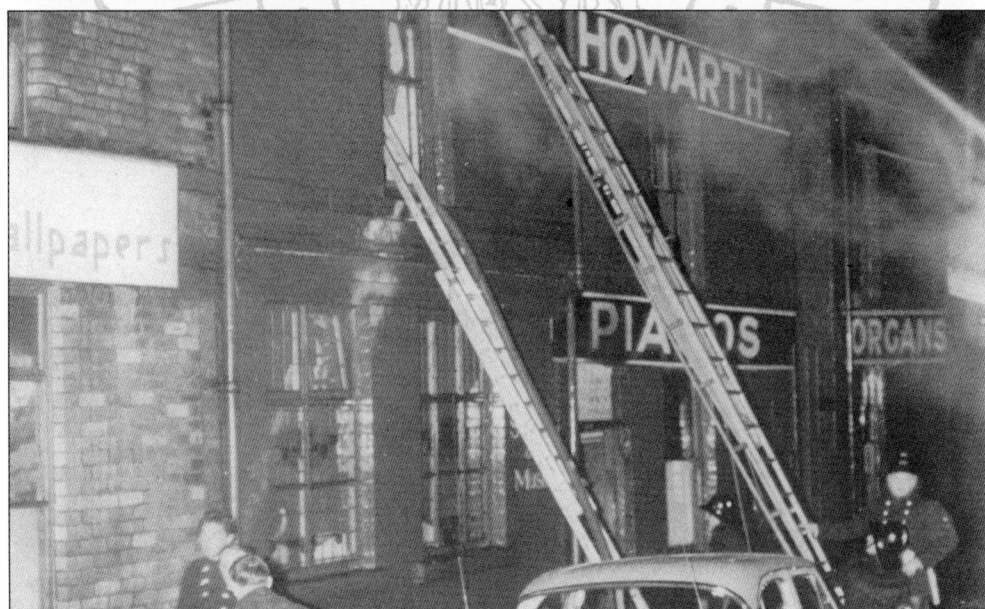

Top Storey Club fire, May 1961

Top Storey Club fire, May 1961

Top Storey Club fire, May 1961

Top Storey Club fire, May 1961

The premises, estimated to be about 150 years old, had been a warehouse and now comprised ground floor offices and workshop, first floor clock rooms and stock rooms, and top floor club rooms – hence the title. Although the building was three floors on the frontage with Crown Street, there were a further two floors below street level. This gave the long side of the building a total of five floors and a height of 60 ft. The River Croal flowed past this side of the building in a stone lined channel.

Shortly after 11 pm, a call was received to the club. On arrival, the Brigade found the staircase at the end of the entrance passage and ground floor workshop well alight, and flames were also issuing from top floor windows. Eight persons had either leapt or fallen the 60 ft from the floor into the darkness below. Some fell on the river banking, others were swept away by the strong current – only three survived the drop.

The Brigade attacked the fire from the entrance passage and pitched a turntable ladder to the top floor riverside window, but the fire was of such intensity that it was impossible to enter. There was no sight or sound of further occupants, but the Brigade worked furiously on the assumption that persons may have been trapped in the building. Further attempts were made to get in at the rear of the building via a top floor loading door, but working from the ladder was extremely difficult as it had to be pitched almost vertically, due to vehicles parked in the narrow alley. It was later found that this door could not, in any case, be opened in the normal manner because an extra floor had been laid on top of the original one, but the door had not been trimmed off, thus the door was held shut by the floor. Two further attempts to get in through windows either side of the loading door were made, but both windows had been bricked up behind the glass. Entrance was finally gained through the ground floor workshop where the fire had originated, and from the entrance staircase. Firemen battled their way up to the blazing staircase to the top storey and, as the smoke and steam cleared, the full impact of the tragedy hit them. At the bar end of the club room a further fourteen victims lay piled on the floor. In all, 19 people (11 men and eight women) died in the disaster. This was the largest number of civilians killed since World War II. This tragic loss occurred in circumstances over which the Brigade had no control.

The Licensing Bill was being debated in the Commons about the time of the tragedy and a wave of public opinion, plus the active support of Bolton MPs, brought amendments to the Bill, which gave Fire Authorities power to inspect club premises and object to the issue or renewal of a club registration on the grounds of fire risks. Prior to this fire, Authorities could only advise and recommend and, in the case of the Top Storey Club, this had been done.

Road traffic accident, Bury Old Road, Bolton

Mayor's Sunday Parade, 1962

W. H. 8000, last shout, 1963

When the Brigade was re-established in 1948, a Fire Prevention Department was created and, over the years, the work of the Department had increased in both scope and importance. The Factories' Act 1961 and the Offices, Ships and Railway Premises' Act 1963, contained sections relating to means of escape in case of fire, and the implementation of this legislation tremendously increased the work load of the Department. The Head of the Department was Assistant Divisional Officer, Frank E. Nuttall, who was considered to be a founder member in fire prevention circles. His devotion to the work earned him a British Empire Medal in 1962.

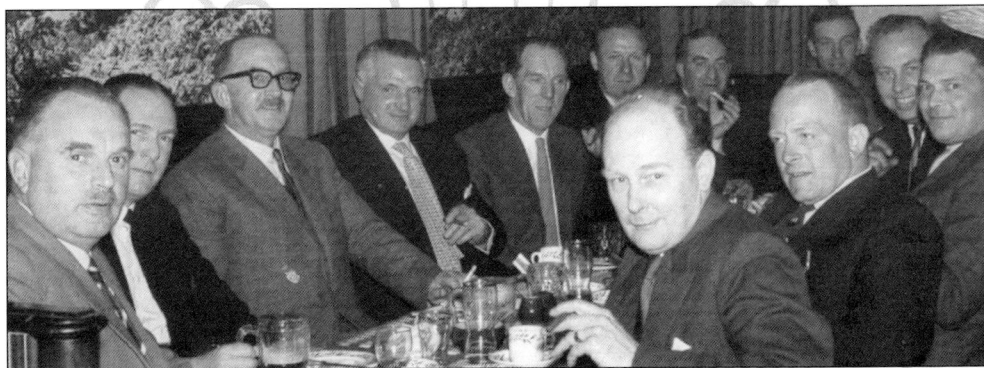

ADO F. E. Nuttall BEM, farewell dinner, 194

In 1964, he left the Brigade to become Senior Instructor, later Chief Instructor, of the Fire Prevention Wing at the Fire Service Technical College, Morton in Marsh.

Lancashire CFB 1st road race, 1964. Bolton's winning team J. Lawton, B. Robinson, A. McCann.

Road race winner Fm. V. Regan and DCO H. Hampson

Fm. J. Lannon retirement, 1965

Special service call rescue of a young lady from farm pit

The team of the 1960s. Back row, left to right: W. Stallard, R. Wilkinson, R. Cook, D. Hayes, R. McClelland, D. Barlow. Front row, left to right: G. Bowes, W. Hart, P. Riley, D. Bevin, R. Howarth.

Fm. Bill Rimmer's retirement

Bolton FB golf team at national golf match, Llandudno 1966

Sept '66

Retirement of deputy chief, H. C. Hampson

Retirement of deputy chief, H. C. Hampson

Shop fire, St. George's Road

A. Holmes Ltd, Saville Street waste paper warehouse, 1966

Bolton fire brigade TTL GLW421 Last run. SubO L. Fogg

In the sixties, Bolton town centre traffic conditions, particularly at peak periods, gradually worsened causing some delay in attendance times. It was also becoming increasingly hazardous to turn out directly on to Marsden Road. Initially a fireman ran into the carriageway waving a red lamp, whilst another fireman went out to warn passing pedestrians. In later year, fixed flashing warning lights were sited on the approach to the station and control staff could regulate the traffic light to facilitate safer turn outs. There was also the problem of appliances returning to the station having to be reversed in across the carriageway, as there was no rear entrance to the appliance room due to the front and rear of the building being built on different levels.

The solution to these problems was to building, first, a sub-station in the north of the town and, second, a new main Headquarters Station – the North Station (a three bay single storey building) conveniently sited on the Ring Road. It was officially open on 30th March 1967, by the Mayor, Alderman Mrs. Nora Vickers JP, and contained a modern work shop, and instructional and recreational facilities. The position of the Station meant quicker attendance to calls in the northern parts of the Brigade's turn out area.

Around this time, Bolton entered a team in a five-mile road race in Lancashire County Fire Brigade. First race, Bolton took first prize. In later years, Bolton had many successes and became a byword in Fire Service sporting circles.

Bolton Road Race. DCFO AL Archer presenting medals 1967

Holden Vale Manufacturing Ltd fire, May 1967

Holden Vale Manufacturing Ltd fire, May 1967

TTL Training SubO Aston in charge. Left to right: Fm. J. Pilkington, SubO Aston, Fm. Baxendale, Fm. K. Eckersly, Fm. D. Clarke.

1968 proved to be an eventful year for the Brigade. In February, the Deputy Chief, Mr. Alan Archer, who had previously served at Coventry, returned there as Deputy Chief. He was succeeded by Mr. J.E. Slack, a Divisional Officer from Leicester City Fire Brigade. Mr. T. Regan was promoted to Deputy.

As an economy measure, the Government decided to disband the Civil Defence organizations, including the Auxiliary Fire Service. Whilst the local AFS had never been numerically very strong, the "hard core" were keen and enthusiastic volunteers. Much resentment was around at the Government's decision but, despite appeals from AFS members to carry on, they were officially "stood down" on 31st March.

Tragedy struck the Brigade on 16th April, when a junior Officer was killed on a special service call. This was to the old Brackley Colliery where three young girls had become trapped in a drift shaft after climbing through a small hole in the roof of the building that covered the head of the sloping shaft. Fire crews from Farnworth and Bolton responded to the call and, on arrival, located the hole, which had to be made bigger to allow them to enter. Some members of the crews were affected by the atmosphere and breathing apparatus was donned. Two of the children were handed out, then the firemen got into difficulties. A Mine's Rescue Team arrived and got out the remaining child, plus the firemen. One of the Bolton crew, Leading Fireman Jack Liptrott, collapsed in the shaft and, as he slumped, his face mask came off. He was removed out into the fresh air and given artificial respiration but efforts to revive him and the children failed. Three other firemen who had been affected fully recovered, after hospital treatment.

LFm. J. Liptrot. Final parade.

Leading Fireman Liptrott was given a full service funeral. Almost the entire Brigade and service colleagues from afar, paraded outside the station to pay their last respects to their comrade, as the wreath covered fire engine carrying the coffin, draped with the Union Jack, passed by. Leading Fireman Liptrott's death revealed an anomaly in the service pension conditions. The Firemen's Pension Scheme had recently been amended to provide an enhanced pension and lump sum gratuity to the dependents of firemen who died through injuries received during fire fighting duties whilst attempting to save life. It came as a shock to the Service to learn that this would not be paid to the firemen who died through injuries received at a "special service" call as distinct from fire fighting duties. Representations were made to the Home Office by the Fire Brigade Union, the Fire Services Committee of the Associations of Municipal Corporations, and Bolton's MP, and a year long fight followed which culminated in a call for the national boycott of all "special service" calls from 1st July 1969. Thankfully, this did not materialise as, in June, the Home Office announced that "special service" calls would be included in the pension amendments.

Retirement of CFO R. C. Bentley, 1968

Chief Officer R.C. Bentley retired on 31st October, having completed 45 years in the Fire Service. He started as a messenger in 1923, then became an Auxiliary Firemen. In 1930 he was appointed to the whole time staff, and rose through the ranks to become Chief of Bolton when the Service was de-nationalised. He served as Chief Officer for over 20 years and, when his father's service in taken into account (he was Bolton's Chief for 22 years), between them they served well over 60 years.

The man chosen to succeed Mr. Bentley was Mr. Gilbert A. Hodgkinson, Chief Officer of Dewsbury. He entered the Service at Birmingham in 1946, following service with the RAF prior to becoming Chief at Dewsbury, he was deputy Chief at Carlisle. Shortly after his appointment, the plans for the building of the new station were passed and the new Chief was determined that the facilities and equipment would be of the highest standard, consistent with a progressive, efficient Brigade.

The Mayor, Cllr. Herbert Glynn presents long service medal at Bolton, November 1969. Left to right: HM Inspector C. N. Bidgood, StnOs Airey, Hilton, Holt, SubOs Burtonwood, Dore, Fm. Cornwell.

By the end of 1969, the annual number of calls the Brigade received had more than doubled the 1959 figure to over 2,400. This broadly followed the national trend where the number of calls had approximately doubled each decade since de-nationalisation and has led to strenuous efforts by Brigades to make the public and industry more fire conscious.

Officers get together, 1969. Left to right: Do D. Smith, StnO A. Airey, StnO W. Holt.

The End of an Era - 1972-1974

The Deputy Chief Officer, Mr. T. Regan, retired in November 1972, having completed 33 years' service. He joined the pre-war Auxiliary Fire Service and, following a period of war time service at Horwich, returned to Bolton where he rose through the ranks to become Deputy Chief in 1969. A dedicated officer, he will be long remembered for his dry sense of humour and his knack of producing the most graphic phrase to fit any situation. Divisional Officer, D.L. Smith, was promoted to Deputy Chief Officer.

Bolton Fire Station, Moor Lane, Bolton. Appliance room, 1973.

H.M.I. 1973

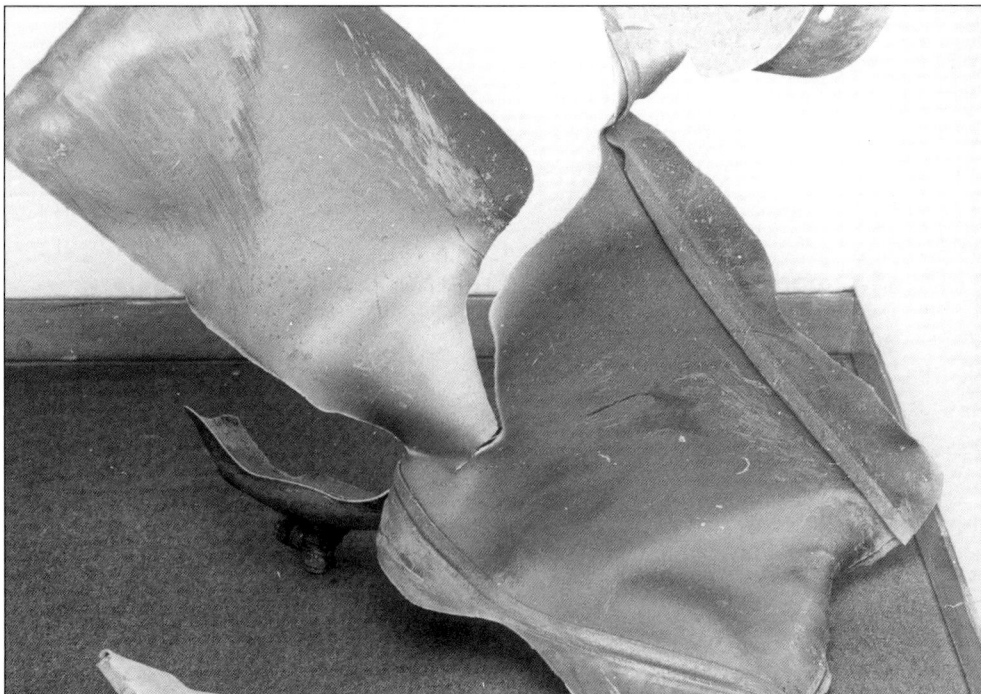

Explosion and fire at office block, Bolton. Calor Gas Art?

Visitors from Europe to main fire station 1973

Quite apart from the increasing number of emergency calls dealt with, the years 1972 and 1973 saw an increase in Brigade activity. The recommendations of the Cunningham Report regarding the modules of training and further involvement in fire prevention duties, were implemented. This training was designed to enable firemen to become fully qualified by the end of their four years of service, thus entitling them to a higher rate of pay. Men with more than four years service also had to reach the qualifying standard.

A system of using operational crews on appliances (in radio contact so that they could answer emergency calls), to carry out fire prevention inspections on a wide range of premises was commenced. This has meant a total involvement of operational personnel in fire prevention work and heralds a change in the role of the Fire Service to that of a Fire Prevention Service.

Ex-Chief Officer, R.C. Bentley, died in November 1973.Regrettably, in latter years, his health had not been good and for one who had served the town so long and so well, he deserved a better retirement.

One of the effects of local Government reorganisation was that Bolton Fire Brigade would lose its individuality and become part of a much larger service, administered by the new Greater Manchester Council. By the end of 1973, arrangements were well in hand to effect the changeover. Naturally enough, this was an uneasy time within the service. In all walks of life people show resistance to change and firemen are no exception. Thus the future was viewed with suspicion. It was also difficult to find anyone, either amongst firemen or citizens of the town, who were in favour of the break up of the old Authorities. Consequently, they were left wondering how it all happened.

Most of the serving officers and HQ staff, early 1974

A farewell dinner-dance was held at the Central Fire Station on 16th March 1974. Amongst the 350 guests attending were many former members, including Mr. Frank Brocklehurst, who had served at the Coronation Street Station as a messenger boy 1899. Also present were Miss Mary Jones and her sister, Mrs. Elsie Smith (Superintendent Jones' daughters, who had been amongst the first families to live on the Marsden Road Station, opened 1899). The Mayor, Mayoress, other civic dignitaries, and one of He Majesty's Inspector of Fire Services, also attended. After dinner, the Mayor paid tribute to the work of the Brigade in its many years of service to the town. The Chief replied by saying how proud he had been to have the Command and that, regrettably, he had had the distinction of being the last Chief Officer of the Brigade. Characteristically, the dance that followed the dinner was interrupted by a "turn out", which proved to be a malicious call.

As the changeover date (1st April) drew nearer, a feeling of anti-climax crept over the Brigade. A tremendous amount of preparation had taken place in all aspects of administration to ensure the least disruption to the Service. Now the general attitude was, "let's get it over with and get the new Service off the ground".

Bolton fire brigade's last parade, April 1974. CFO G. Hodkinson. Left to right, 1st Row: DO C. Hobbs, DO A. Airey, DO D. Smith, DO N. Hilton. 2nd row: StnOs J. Ratcliffe, G. Bowes, R. Wilkinson, ADOs F. Booth, W. Holt, StnOs J. Walsh, P. Riley. 3rd row: L. W`rd, D. Winrow, R. McClelland, J. Fenny, T. Shepherd, W. Stallad, A. Davies, P. Jones, M. Carren, N. Tillbrook, J. Roscoe, J. Hardman, G. Fox, J. Yates, K. Loftus, J. Walsh, J. Swift.

The last shift of the Bolton Fire Brigade came on duty on Sunday evening, 31st March, and the first shift of Station B20 of the Greater Manchester County Fire Service reported at 9 am on 1st April. At the "changeover" parade, it was "hats off" and three cheers for the old Brigade before they dismissed. Thus ended more than 170 years of service to the people of Bolton by the Bolton Fire Brigade. The Fire Service, always sensitive of its image, know that it will be judged in the future, as it has been in the past, on two counts. Namely, on the standard of service that it provides, and on the quality of those who serve in it.

1st April 1974. GMC Birthday fire!
Paper warehouse, Bridgeman Place.

End Note: The New Fire Service

On 1st April 1974, due to the local Government's reorganisation, the Brigades of Manchester, Salford, Stockport, Wigan, Bolton, Bury, Rochdale, and Oldham, ceased to exist and became the new Greater Manchester County Fire Service. Covering an area of some 500 square miles, serving a population of more than two and a half million people.

Situated on Bolton Road, Swinton, the new County Headquarters opened in November 1979, and it is the nerve centre of the Brigade. Housed in the complex are various support departments essential to the smooth running of an efficient, modern Fire Service. Included are Operations and Training, Fire Prevention and Investigation, Transport and Administrative Support Sections, and a large section devoted to computerised Command and Control. This Fire Service Control is the most modern, to date, in the country and makes use of some of today's most up to date computer systems.

Bibliography

Airey, A. & Cook, R. K. (1974) *The Old Brigade.* Blackshaw, Sykes & Morris.

Bolton Fire Brigade (1800 - 1930) *Log Books & Committee Minutes & Reports.*

Bolton Fire Brigade (1948 - 1974) *Chief Officer's Reports.*

Bolton Fire Brigade (1961) *Top Storey Club Fire & Fire Investigation Reports.*

Farrell, J. E. (1996) *As It Happened.* Unpublished Text.